Inside the
Nonprofit
Boardroom

What You Need to Know for Satisfaction and Success

by Charles William Golding
with Craig W. Stewart

Foreword by
William H. Gates, Sr.

Illustrated by
Tedrowe Watkins

Second Edition

Documentary Media

Seattle, Washington

Inside the Nonprofit Boardroom

What You Need to Know for Satisfaction and Success

Printed in Canada

Inside the Nonprofit Boardroom is printed on Rolland Enviro 100% post-consumer waste
recycled paper, Forest Stewardship Council certified.

Authors: Charles William Golding with Craig W. Stewart
Illustrator: Tedrowe Watkins
Editors: Don Graydon, Sherri Schultz, and Judy Gouldthorpe
Designer: Paul Langland
Executive Editor: Barry Provorse
Publisher: Petyr Beck

Library of Congress Cataloging-in-Publication Data

Golding, Charles William.
Inside the nonprofit boardroom : what you need to know for satisfaction and success /
Charles William Golding with Craig W. Stewart ; illustrated by Tedrowe Watkins. --
2nd ed.
     p. cm.
ISBN 978-0-295-98932-7
1. Boards of directors. 2. Nonprofit organizations--Management.
I. Stewart, Craig W., 1941- II. Title.
HD2745.G65 2009
658.4'22--dc22
2008050083

Documentary Media LLC
3250 41st Avenue SW
Seattle, WA 98116
(206) 935-9292

Documentary Media publishes books for corporate and institutional clients across North
America. For more information about our titles and services, contact us at the address listed
above, or view our website at www.documentarymedia.com.

Distributed by University of Washington Press, PO Box 50096, Seattle, WA 98145-5096.
www.washington.edu/uwpress

IN MEMORY OF CHARLES WILLIAM GOLDING, gentleman, scholar, mentor, and friend. Thanks for sharing your love, wisdom, and courage with us while you were here.
Your words and spirit continue to sustain and inspire us.

Charles William Golding, 1931-2004

Table of Contents

Foreword

The continuing failure of boards in the nonprofit sector to grow and lead has resulted in enormous stress on the public to whom they are accountable. Can we who serve as trustees emphatically say we are successfully performing our primary leadership and fiduciary responsibilities to sustain and grow our organizations? Sadly, too often the answer is no. In many cases, boards and trustees don't understand the responsibilities involved. All too often, the lack of engagement and underutilization of passion and skills have contributed to failures.

Is there an intersection between satisfaction and success as a board and trustee? I am convinced there is, and that the work in which we are engaged must be meaningful to result in positive outcomes for the organizations we serve. In short, the work of boards and trustees must focus on successfully reaching the mission and objectives of our organizations. This is indeed not work for the faint of heart. Boards represent both the organizations they serve and the larger public composed of the individuals who invest in their trust by providing donations and other kinds of support. This lack of focus often results in a handoff to the chief executive, who ends up with inadequate input and inadequate resources. Boards should no longer depend upon the sole leadership of the chief executive.

In truth, the more collaborative that chief executives and boards are, the more successful the organization.

Bill Golding and Craig Stewart have written a very useful and no-nonsense primer for folks who serve or want to serve on nonprofit boards. They have unequivocally spelled out the obligations of the board. All too often these duties have been treated as second-class commitments, subject to being set aside in favor of most any personal distraction that comes along. All of what they have written has validity today. Nonetheless, there are new emerging models and thinking on the subject of governance that board members would be well advised to take seriously.

To achieve success today requires close and transparent teamwork between the board and chief executive. Governance simply works best as a partnership where work is shared. This will require more open and honest discussion, which all too often has tended to occur only in times of crisis.

In the addendum, Craig offers some thoughts about the changing dynamics in the nonprofit boardroom that will contribute to your achieving satisfaction and success as a board and trustee.

William H. Gates, Sr.

Why this handbook

A successful and sophisticated guy who ran a large regional architectural firm was invited to join the board of a nonprofit corporation. We were talking together about it when suddenly he said, a little sheepishly, in a slightly conspiratorial voice, *"What does a board really do?"*

Very good question. Read on for the answer. This handbook is meant for that man, and it's meant for you: a trustee or prospective trustee of a nonprofit organization. It gets right down to the nitty-gritty of what a board is and what a trustee is. It gives an inside look at what boards and trustees really do and reveals how you can be at your most effective. It gives pointed tips on meetings, elections, and everything else you need to know as you enter the nonprofit boardroom.

Each of the two million nonprofits in this country needs someone to oversee its work—and that "someone" is usually a board of trustees. Millions of Americans serve on nonprofit boards, but few trustees know what's expected of them when they take on this volunteer role. That's where this handbook comes in.

Try spending half an hour with this booklet. In short order it can make you a more effective trustee, regardless of the size or purpose of the nonprofit organization you serve.

1
What is a board?

A board is a group of people charged with the ultimate responsibility for the health, preservation, and progress of an organization. *It does not run anything.* It works with the people who do. A board should reflect the population it serves.

COMPANIONSHIP

2

What is a trustee?

People with board responsibilities for nonprofit organizations—charities, schools, hospitals, foundations, religious or
community groups, and other causes of all kinds—are generally called *trustees*. Sometimes they are called directors, or some
name specific to the cause served—for example, deacons in
the Baptist Church. But ninety-eight times out of a hundred,
they are called trustees.

A trustee—that's you—is a member of the board. You
hold the operations, functions, and the very existence of
the organization in trust for the people who contribute to it
and for those who benefit from it.

What does "in trust" mean? It means that you nurture,
care for, and protect the entire organization.

3

Big boards, little boards

Each kind of nonprofit organization will have its own type of board, ranging from very active to downright passive.

Type flows from size. For example, metropolitan nonprofit corporations for the arts—symphony orchestras, museums, opera and ballet companies—tend to have large boards, with twenty-five to thirty-five members, often making for a relatively passive body that functions by committee. Small and hyperactive boards are commonly found in nonprofit corporations that provide essential public services, such as volunteer fire departments or rural water districts; the board may have only three to five members. Religious organizations, churches, or synagogues often fall somewhere in the middle, with perhaps twelve to fifteen people on the board.

Fact of life: The large board is created for one major purpose, and don't kid yourself otherwise. It's simple. The organization wants more people who can get money and give money.

A board's involvement in detail is in inverse ratio to its size: the bigger the board, the less involvement in day-to-day details; the smaller the board, the more involvement. The danger here is that small boards can end up doing what they shouldn't do: manage. Our local library has a politically appointed board of five persons. Until recently, the board made the mistake of engaging in micromanagement. Similarly, a public school board near us gets into operating details that belong to management and gums it up more often than not.

Private foundations commonly have a small board and a high-quality professional staff. The board is able to stay focused on the big picture, while the professional staff executes 100 percent of the details.

4
Why have a board in the first place?

IT'S THE LAW

Let's back up for a minute. Why have a board at all? Here are three reasons.

REASON ONE: THE LAW REQUIRES IT.

Each organization is, or should be, a legal entity. All nonprofit organizations—including churches, synagogues, civic enterprises such as a water district, and charity or social causes—are formed by legal documents, or should be. If yours is not legally formed, cause it to happen, or get out.

Don't try to go on the cheap and buy drugstore forms for creating a corporation. Get a good, respected lawyer. Period. You can't afford it? Yes, you can. Go to a good law firm and ask them to do it for nothing. That's called pro bono—short for *pro bono publico*, meaning "for the good of the public." Most lawyers, especially in medium-size and smaller firms, will do it. They like the publicity, and that's how they get business. Or ask a sole practitioner. My brother was in practice by himself for forty years, daily washing the feet of the unwashed, and he was always willing to help a good cause. You'll find someone like him. They're out there. What you *cannot* afford is *not* to be fully legal.

Generally these organizations are formed under a state law called the Uniform Nonprofit Corporation Act. The vast majority of states have adopted this act. If your state doesn't have this uniform law, it will have something that is a twin, or at least a first cousin.

The Uniform Nonprofit Corporation Act states, "The affairs of a corporation shall be managed by a board of directors. . . . " But don't let the word "managed" confuse you. It's a misuse of the word. As you already know, good boards do *not* manage. They delegate that function to a person called an executive director, or sometimes called a president.

Many nonprofit corporations accept donations from the public, and these donations are usually tax deductible. It's no secret that people want to be able to deduct what they give. So be sure that gifts to your corporation are tax deductible. How? See a tax lawyer and get the corporation qualified as one for which contributions are deductible. You'll hear people in the nonprofit sector say, "We're a 501(c)(3)." What this means is that their organization has qualified under the Internal Revenue Code, Section 501, subparagraph c, sub-subparagraph 3. Gobbledygook, but *required* gobbledygook. If your organization is not a 501(c)(3), contributions are normally not deductible.

Since the law requires a board, we don't need any other reason. But there are two more reasons, both rooted in common sense and good judgment.

Reason Two: The management needs it.

The board can provide a sounding board—a place for management to get feedback, advice, and, most important, creative ideas stemming from a fresh perspective.

Such an atmosphere of creativity and cooperation is not quite as rare as a perfect day in Seattle in the damp month of June. It can and does occur. When a board becomes a true and solid sounding place for management, and when management has both the courage and the sense to listen, the positive effects can be remarkable on both sides.

Reason Three: The people want it.

A nonprofit board should give all the people connected with an organization the sense of security that comes with knowing that someone is overseeing things. People want to feel that someone is paying attention to what is going on. That's the job of the board.

5
Qualities of a trustee

Every trustee should possess the following:

Integrity. Be a moral force to keep the organization on the straight and narrow, doing nothing improper at any time.

Judgment. Help the board choose the right course of action.

Perspective. Help the board and the organization keep their balance through both adversity and acclaim.

Courage. Hold firm to your belief in the organization and in the steps it must take to fulfill its mission.

Creativity. Stimulate other board members and the professional staff with constructive ideas that challenge everyone to think creatively for the organization.

Dependability. Show up at all times when needed.

Stability. Be known as one who is always prepared.

Focus. Keep yourself and the entire board focused on the purpose of the organization.

Sensitivity to Diversity. Demonstrate respect for minority and socio-economic diversity issues and a willingness to deal with them.

Humility. Serving on a board is not about you. It's about doing all you can to help the organization carry out its mission.

If you or your board determines other necessary qualities, fine. Each organization will require, after reflection, one or two other qualities in its trustees. Get people who have them. However, if you satisfy just the list above, you will have done 90 percent of the job. We know this much: if you accept trustees who lack most of these qualities, you will be getting the wrong people who may lead you down the wrong path, and no other qualities will correct the deficiencies.

6

The passionate trustee

A trustee of a nonprofit board makes some strong personal commitments to the organization in accepting the position. These commitments must be maintained during the entire time of service.

BELIEF IN THE MISSION

Each trustee must have a heartfelt belief in the mission of the organization. The best of all worlds is when this belief is truly a passion—for music, for example, or for the church or synagogue, or for the environment, art, or theater. You may not want a person on the library board who never reads a book, or a couch potato on the board of the wilderness adventures group.

You want someone who feels, who burns, with a desire for the cause. The ideal situation is when the trustee experiences the intensity of the cause in his or her head, heart, and stomach. People are most productive when involved in something they genuinely care about. If you are asked to be a trustee and you don't feel this way, then do yourself and the organization a big favor: don't accept.

MONEY: RAISING IT, GIVING IT

Most charitable organizations count on trustees to assist in raising money. As a trustee you are expected, if not required, to give money yourself. And you are clearly expected to call upon others to give money.

"You know, I'm just not comfortable asking people for money."

I've heard that one a thousand times. Okay, then don't be a trustee. Because trustees generally have to raise money, unless the nonprofit is a public entity. Now, before you walk away in a huff, listen to something. My former business partner, one of the greatest fund-raisers anyone could ever find, educated me. "Bill," he said, "remember that you're doing these people a favor. There are so many people with money to give, but they don't know *where* to give it, or even *how*." He was dead right. It just took me a long time to learn it.

How much you yourself give may influence others—but it probably won't. After all, it's very rare that someone is gutsy enough to say to you, "How much did *you* give?" But even if you can't give a lot, you must give something. Don't be embarrassed if your gift is small in dollars. Not everyone is wealthy and—thank God—the actual amount of money you give is not often a criterion for nonprofit board membership. You say you still feel uncomfortable because you can't give as much as some other trustees? Nonsense. Just be a better trustee.

The important thing is to help raise some money. You'll find that if you give generously yourself, by your own financial standards, then asking other people to give generously becomes a lot easier.

Here's something to watch out for: a lot of charitable and cultural boards of long standing have lost their way because they are used as social vehicles. When that occurs, board seats have distinct, understood price tags. I remember a luncheon meeting with a well-known person in our city, my sole purpose being to enlist his help in placing a certain person on a particular board. My nominee was eminently qualified as a trustee and wanted the affiliation on his list of credits. I got right down to the nitty-gritty:

"What's the going rate for a seat on the board?" I asked.

"Five thousand a year, the same as the symphony, but I understand several organizations like the symphony, opera, and ballet are going to increase that to around ten thousand next year."

Sound crazy? Try Chicago, Los Angeles, or the Big Apple, and I'll bet that number can be multiplied by three, or five, or ten or more.

7
The rewards

Serving as a nonprofit trustee is a volunteer job. But that
doesn't mean there aren't rewards.

HONOR

It is the honor of the position, of being asked, of serving,
of having it known that you serve, that is generally the greatest
motivator for people who volunteer for nonprofit boards.
This is an honest motive, and should not be looked at askance.

If the organization is doing a good job, its aura will attract
good people—a fine situation for both the nonprofit and
its board.

"For the honor," Aristotle wrote in *Nicomachean Ethics,*
"depends more upon the people who pay it than upon the
person to whom it is paid."

That, dear reader, is a classic. Please *think* carefully about it.

COMPENSATION

SATISFACTION

The honor may be enough to motivate you to join a board, and enough to keep you there for a while, but for you to perform at your best, there must be more. At the core must be pleasure in what you are doing. There must be inner satisfaction that your efforts mean something—not just to others, but also to you.

That says something good about us, not something shallow. For unless you derive satisfaction from serving on the board of a nonprofit organization, your interest will wane and you will no longer be contributing your best work.

RELATIONSHIPS

One of the first questions a prospective trustee asks when approached about serving is "Who else sits on the board?" People are alike in this regard. They want to know who is going to be there with them. Like begets like. Quality people, well respected for their abilities, draw other quality people.

If you enjoy the relationships you have with the other people on the board, you will be inclined to serve well and long. The chance for these associations helps motivate people to accept the job and to stay with it.

RELATIONSHIPS

MONEY

There was a time during the self-centered 1980s when the thesis was advanced that the younger generation would not serve on the nonprofit boards of the future without pay. "Yuppies expect pay," it was said. Yes, and perhaps they expected the eighties to go on forever.

And now the greedy 1990s are also gone, the decade of soaring stock prices and instant millionaires, and we are starting to get back to basics. One of the most attractive basics is service to other people. And God knows we are ready for it, even desperately in need of it. If you have, you give: money, talent, and time. You serve.

No, monetary pay will never be a factor. The compensation is in different forms, as it should be.

8
What does a board do?

The functions of a board can be many and varied, but should always include the ones discussed in this section.

REPRESENT THE INTERESTS OF DONORS

The first function of a nonprofit board is to serve and protect the interests of the people who provide the money to support the organization's mission. Selfish? No. If the donors have a focus—for example, a theater and its theatrical presentations— you had better serve that interest, stay focused on the best theater productions, and not somehow get diverted into, say, trying to make videos or films.

This example may be extreme, but the extreme can happen. The professionals hired by an organization can lose sight of what the mission is, especially if they are very good at what they do. Hubris strikes, and they feel that they can never make a mistake. Well, the board is there to be sure of that.

Nonprofit boards clearly must believe in and advance the organization's stated purpose and defend the interests of the people who put up their money to support that purpose. That is as true for a family foundation as it is for a library supported with public tax funds and supplemented by private donors.

Represent the interests of recipients

The identical twin of the first responsibility is to represent the interests of the recipients. That is exactly what the donors want you to do, so there is no conflict.

Nonprofit boards serve the constituents who benefit from the organization's purpose. For example, a water district serves the homes and businesses that get water; a school, the students who attend; a theater company, the performers and the audiences; a foundation, all the people who receive grant money.

Keep things legal

The board must ensure that the activities of the organization are legal and in compliance in all respects. It's a critical duty, because illegality can seep into any place like water penetrating sand.

Some board member will usually say that this is a job for a lawyer—and thus a lawyer should be named to the board. No.

How will you know if activities are legal? For one thing, try using your common sense. If a report sounds fishy, follow the smell and keep asking questions. You'll find the answer.

I remember a private school that tried to allow parents to take a tax deduction for tuition payments. The IRS informed the school that if it continued to hold that position, it would lose its 501(c)(3) status—that is, its IRS status as an institution that can accept tax-deductible donations. The board acted quickly to strike the objectionable language despite unfavorable reactions from a few parents. For the board, the important thing was to keep the institution on the straight and narrow.

The real key is the chief executive officer hired by the board. He or she sets the tone for the institution's legal standards. My father-in-law was a Greek immigrant and a typical American success story, and with his uncommon common sense he taught me a ton. "Bill," he would say, "a corporation is like a fish. It rots from the head first." And that includes nonprofit corporations.

Keep things moral

Board members must make it their business to see that the
nonprofit corporation they serve performs at the highest
ethical and moral level. During consultations with nonprofit
boards, I'm frequently asked: "What is the definition of
morality in a nonprofit corporation's performance?" The
answer is simple and straightforward: the conduct of all
activities by all persons representing the corporation in any
way, at any time, must be right and proper. The actions must
be—and must be viewed as—ethical.

Let me give a real-life example. When James Baker was
White House chief of staff, he asked that a door be added to
his office so he could step outside into a little private space
to feed and water the birds, a hobby he enjoyed. The cost
of the work was about $1,500. He paid for it himself. Another
official told Baker that since his office was being remodeled
anyway, the payment was unnecessary because it was really
a government expense. Baker just smiled and said, "It may be,
but what counts is the *perception* of what it is."

Both the conduct and the perception of that conduct must
pass the test of morality.

Hire and help the paid chief executive

The board is responsible for hiring the person who runs the organization. This paid chief executive is commonly called the executive director. Likewise, the board fires him or her if it doesn't work out.

A good board stays out of the details of operations. Otherwise, well-intended actions become disruptive and confusing for everyone. Even worse, the board loses its perspective.

If one or two trustees start nit-picking, and you have a strong board president, he or she will say in open forum, diplomatically of course, "That issue is, in my judgment, a management issue and not one within the province of the board, so we'll move on. If you wish to talk to me further about it, we can do so after the meeting." That way, trustee meddling is cut off with one swat.

As the board must assist the executive director, so the executive director must assist the board. In the best of all worlds, the executive director should be able to use the board as a forum for open and candid discussion. The board and the director should be able to ask any questions, with neither side feeling threatened or intimidated. It doesn't always work that way, but it should. Try it.

APPROVE OVERALL CONCEPTS

The board should approve the basic conceptual objectives of the organization's strategic plan. Only in the very earliest days of a nonprofit should the board attempt to formulate strategy. Otherwise, let the executive director outline it.

Admittedly the line is finely drawn. Mr. Justice Potter Stewart expressed the opinion that while he could not define pornography, "I know it when I see it." You will know which side of the line you are on—conceptual approval or involvement in the details—when you see it. How? You will be comfortable one way, uncomfortable the other.

Some of the broad questions a board asks when discussing the strategic plan are: What activities are we really involved in? What activities *should* we be involved in? Is our overall plan realistic? Is it too ambitious, or perhaps not ambitious enough?

STRATEGIC PLANNING

ESTABLISH POLICIES

The board establishes all policies for the nonprofit and makes
certain that the organization adheres to those policies. What is
a policy? It is a statement of *belief* describing the organization's
specific goal, and sometimes how it wants to achieve it. Some
examples of policies are: on financial issues such as audited
statements and portfolio investment guidelines; on fund-raising
issues such as what kind of gifts will or will not be accepted;

on issues affecting any phase of the organization's objectives
and/or activities; and on interaction between various
communities and the organization. Depending on *what* the
organization does, policies obviously vary. For example, a
school or college has policies on scholarships; a foundation on
what type of grant applications will be considered and how
grants shall be made; a hospital on whether or not to have an
"open door" policy to admit all patients. Policies of large
organizations are usually generated by board committees and
presented to the board as a whole. Small and/or new nonprofit
boards form their own policies as circumstances arise.

SUMMING IT UP

A board's principal obligation is to serve the organization's
cause, its donors, and its recipients. To carry out its obligation,
the board receives and digests information. The board observes,
evaluates, and consults with the paid professional who runs
the organization day to day. The board asks questions in order
to understand more fully what is going on in the organization.
The board develops an interaction among its members
to achieve that wonderful condition known as synergy.
And the board makes the most of its individual and group
intuitive powers.

   In short, a board does anything, and everything, that is
moral and legal to assist the organization.

9

What does a trustee do?

A trustee has what is known as fiduciary responsibility. This
means that you, as a trustee, hold the organization in the palm
of your hand, like a little bird, and must protect it and help
it to grow. Here are some simple and basic ways you can go
about meeting that big responsibility.

ATTEND MEETINGS

Pretty simple, but you do have to decide what your priorities
are. If you serve on a board, its meetings are high up on your
list. You cannot participate unless you are present, so you need
to commit yourself to the dates and times of meetings and
be present. If a board meets quarterly, there are no excuses for
absences except death in the family. None.

Small boards always feel compelled to meet a lot—too
much, in fact. They're afraid they'll miss something. Forget it.
At most, a board should meet once every two months.
Otherwise you get tangled up in the details. You will *not*
miss anything—and you will do a better job. The federal

government requires bank boards to meet monthly, which is unnecessary. I know. I did it for twenty years. This is the same government that gave us the savings and loan debacle. The cost to taxpayers? Oh, $50 billion at least, until they stopped counting.

Do homework

Mature boards, or new ones properly managed, present you with materials before the meetings. If your board does not, ask them to do so. When you get the materials in advance, for heaven's sake, read them before the meeting. If you are going to understand and contribute, you must be informed.

It's not necessary to ask questions and refer back to the materials in the meetings to show people that you have done your homework, although that trick does help once in a while. It reminds management and other board members that you are on the job.

The little extras we do without being asked, like helping at home with the daily chores, are what make life work well. So too with board homework: do a little extra.

HOMEWORK

STARE OUT THE WINDOW

Before heading off to each meeting, close your door at home or in the office, take no calls, and permit no interruptions as you sit quietly, stare out of your window, and really think about the organization. What are its problems? What are its opportunities? Be reflective for a good long time. Free yourself to think. You'll be a more focused and effective trustee for it.

THINKING

Stay awake

He drew pictures of his feet. Adjusting his chair back from the table while leaning over the notepad, he could pretend he was writing creative, forward-thinking ideas for the organization while the board meeting droned on.

In reality, he was diverting his mind, lessening the tedium, preventing his own slow death in the afternoon. It occurred at every monthly meeting of the board of trustees of Do Good Things, Unlimited.

He changed his tack and began to draw a picture of the board president, a tall, thin, bald man with big round glasses and the personality of a stone. Whether you like him or not, he mused, President Clinton has a great personality. Why can't every board president emulate Clinton's good side?

The ultimate job of every trustee, he wrote carefully, outlining each word, is to *stay awake!*

Hit the ball back

When presentations are made by management or others to the
board, don't be a sponge. React. Respond. Hit the ball back.
Say something. Compliment. Ask. Clap. Do something.

That is the trick to creating an atmosphere of interest and
possible excitement in the boardroom. When the open
exchange comes, it can be pure poetry. If the atmosphere is
missing, your chance for success diminishes. Your job as a
board member is to help create that atmosphere.

INTEREST

10
The keys to success

Inquisitiveness

Effective trustees make a habit of a couple of simple acts that go a long way toward guaranteeing success on the board.

Ask questions
The successful trustee asks questions. Ask all the questions you have, all the time. The well-functioning board operates in an environment in which the trustees are comfortable asking questions.

What questions? Well, the possibilities are endless. Here are some that come to mind:

"How do we recruit new people to get involved with this board and this organization?"

"Why are we building a huge new main library when the action is either with computers or out in the branches?"

"Can all of our PCs talk to each other on the same network?"

"Why do we always meet at four in the afternoon, when a lot of us are tired?"

"Do we have a shadow organization chart—one that shows backup and possible replacements for our key people? If we do, shouldn't it be made available to at least certain board members?"

"Is the history of our donors in a database? If not, why not? What kind of information can we get about each donor?"

"When was the last time we surveyed our constituents about the effects of our programs?"

"Why isn't there more publicity when we receive a major gift?"

"Why isn't there more news when we create something new and useful?"

"Why do we always meet on the same day?"

You get the idea.

THANK THE STAFF

The successful trustee never forgets to say "thank you" or "great job" or "well done" to management and staff. They will carry these words home and bask in them. That's good.

11

Money and people

The board of a nonprofit organization has to develop
in-depth knowledge of both the finances and the people of
the organization.

KEEPING TRACK OF THE MONEY

Each trustee must receive regular financial statements, review
and analyze them, and understand the accounting methods
employed.

The board of a nonprofit must be more exacting in its
budget approvals and guard finances more closely than
corporate or business boards do. Why? Trouble can come
more quickly. There is generally less staff, or even no staff.
Quite often only limited funds are available to remedy
financial problems.

The small organization is usually at greatest risk. With its
small volunteer board and its small or nonexistent paid staff,
you'd best assume that lights, whistles, and bells have gone off.
The problem will rarely be willful manipulation, theft,
or wrongdoing. Rather, it will be neglect, postponement,

basic mistakes, irregularity—and, quite frequently, just plain ignorance of what to do. Your job is to correct the situation. Force the issue. Do whatever is necessary, but *pay* an accountant or bookkeeper to set up and maintain a set of books and to prepare and send the financial statements to the trustees.

Any board worth its salt should have an outside accounting firm prepare annual financial statements. They should be audited statements. That means the accounting firm puts its own reputation on the line by stating that the statements are true and correct, based on the firm's independent analysis of the organization's books.

But again, let's deal with the small nonprofit. If audited statements are too expensive, get what are known as compiled statements or reviews. The accountant certifies nothing, simply preparing the financial statements from the organization's books, and so stating. The compiled statements or reviews will be bound, will look very official, and will say to people: "We're trying."

The board should permit debt only in the rarest of instances—perhaps for a specific project for which money from an established source, such as an upcoming capital fund drive, can be counted on and total financing is clearly provided.

Financial Analysis

The organization should never, not ever, be permitted to operate at a deficit. If for some unforeseen reason a deficit occurs one year, the loss must be made up in the next year. Three years in a row and you strike out. Resign. You are not doing your job.

Keeping track of the people

The nonprofit board of trustees has a special function that is not expected of business boards and consequently is often overlooked, especially on the bigger, more mature and sophisticated boards. One or two of the most trusted members of the board need to be responsible for understanding the interpersonal relationships within the organization itself. And what does this mean? It means the trustees study and observe how the various constituencies get along with each other.

For example, does the staff of the local ballet company think well of the creative producers and directors? Do the dancers function well with the staff and the artistic directors? At a school, how does the administration interact with the faculty? Does the faculty respect the administration, and vice versa? I knew of a prestigious independent school where few, if any, faculty members respected anyone in the administration: the head of the school, assistant head, or head of either the upper or lower school. The students were asked how they felt about the head and other members of the administration. The response: "We never see them." The board had no knowledge of this situation, and the results were near disastrous.

Trustees need to understand these interpersonal relationships—without interfering with the leader of the organization. It's a tough job, but it must be done.

12
What the board needs to know

TIMELY INFORMATION

The trustees of a nonprofit organization can function well only with full and correct information. Most of this information comes in the form of materials prepared for each board meeting and from the meetings themselves. Detailed information, plus the meeting agenda, should be received by each trustee at least five full working days in advance of the session.

There is a distinct tendency of nonprofit organizations to ignore this basic rule and to hand out materials at the meetings themselves. That conduct is both rude and unacceptable.

Information should be sent to the board on the following topics.

Finances. Quarterly financial reports are needed, including investment and endowment portfolio analyses. Monthly statements are more *detailed* than the board needs. Of course, if the board meets once every two months, use bimonthly financials. Knowledge of the current financial status is especially critical with nonprofit organizations because their purpose is not to produce a profit, so they may pay insufficient attention to finances. Nonprofit organizations can make huge mistakes in money matters unless there is a clear and broad perspective—and oversight—by the board.

The cause. A nonprofit board should learn new facts or developments about the cause it supports—not just in its own backyard but regionally, nationally, and internationally if its reach is wide.

Recipients. The board needs to know what the recipients of the organization's money, services, or other largesse really think. Recipients might include symphony or ballet audiences, schoolchildren and parents, or people helped by foundation grants. How is this information collected? One family foundation I know is run by a top-flight professional who visits the recipients of its funds and discusses the gifts and their uses, gaining firsthand insight into the people and their points of view. This person travels a lot!

Donors. The board needs to learn about the principal donors to the organization. Some of the trustees should develop personal relationships with major donors, getting to know them face-to-face as human beings.

Management. The board needs to develop knowledge and understanding of the professionals running the operation. What kind of people are they? What motivates them? What do they *really* think?

Physical assets. The board should be conversant, in a general way, with the properties and equipment of the organization as well as technologies used.

Insurance. The board should receive a complete insurance report once a year and examine it broadly for an understanding of the coverage and the costs.

Legal issues. A quick annual review of legal issues by the organization's general counsel is a good idea. The general counsel should not be a member of the board, but that individual should frequently be invited to sit at board meetings.

13

How meetings work

How OFTEN TO MEET

Mature and well-established nonprofit organizations generally
hold quarterly board meetings. So do many of the sophisticated new foundations. Their trustees are busy people with
full lives, and they neither want nor need any more meetings.
If they meet more frequently, they can start getting into too
much detail.

Nonprofit boards can have a tendency to meet too often.
Generally this mistake is due to a lack of steady, firm
leadership. Some trustees use a meeting as an excuse for a
social gathering; some simply don't have enough to do and are
nervous with too many blank spaces on their calendars.
However, monthly meetings sometimes are required. For
example, the Joint Commission on Accreditation of Healthcare
Organizations requires that boards meet monthly.

A young nonprofit organization should probably have its board meet bimonthly—once every two months. Time off for good behavior is a wise policy. Try making the December meeting a shorter one and add some social time. And work out the schedule so you never meet in August; no one does much of anything in August.

A schedule of meetings should be sent to each trustee in November or December, listing all dates and times for the following year. Days of the week may be varied. Monday is not the best day, and Friday is bad for obvious reasons.

WHERE TO MEET

Always hold meetings in the building of the organization. For example, a children's hospital board should meet at the hospital itself. Why? So the people on the staff know that the board is there; so they know the board exists and cares. If a nonprofit corporation has more than one facility, occasional meetings can be scheduled in places other than the principal location. The foundation supporting a library system should meet once or twice a year at branch libraries. Such a meeting is also good for trustees because it forces them to learn about other facilities.

WHAT TIME TO MEET

Meetings should be held at a time that is considered best by general consensus of the board, and that is most often in the afternoon. Businesspeople can finish up their day's work and then concentrate on the board business at hand.

The flip side of the afternoon session is the breakfast meeting, generally scheduled at the ungodly hour of 7:30 A.M. After some years of breakfast meetings, I simply decided that I had had enough. After that, I went to a breakfast gathering only if my business partner was receiving an award plaque. He was a wealthy, active, and vital man, so he received two or three a year. I would show up just as the breakfast dishes were being cleared from the tables, see him get his plaque, quickly congratulate him, and leave. If you insist on holding a breakfast meeting, you will see a constant raising of arms to look at wristwatches. You will never have a relaxed board.

For heaven's sake, start the meeting on time. If someone arrives late, don't stop the meeting to catch them up. They'll get the message.

How LONG?

How long should a meeting last? Common sense gives you the answer. This is not rocket science, you know. Two to two and a half hours is generally the length. A coffee break about halfway through lets people use the facilities, make a phone call, or—best of all—talk among themselves about what has been said at the meeting and what is coming up.

Shorter meetings are better and more focused. Get past the routine stuff in a rapid-fire manner to allow time to discuss, openly and freely, the topics that need the board's emphasis and input. Don't be afraid to have a very quick meeting when it is called for, just as you should also warn people at certain times, in advance of the meeting, that the topics are critical and you hope they will plan to give the time that is necessary.

All of this, of course, relies on strong board leadership. Some people can run a meeting well, and some cannot. Realize that meetings can, and often do, become so routine that they are truly "slow death in the afternoon." If this happens with your board more than once, have the courage to stand up and say so. You will be respected for your candor, and things most likely will change for the better. If they don't, meet with the board president privately. If nothing works, pick your time and just leave the board. I had to do that once. It was painful but necessary.

End the meeting on time. Otherwise you will lose people anyway: they'll just leave or else fall asleep. Respect people's time and don't waste it.

One simple truth should govern a meeting's duration: the mind can absorb only what the bottom can endure.

"The mind can only absorb what the bottom can endure"

Special meetings

Events may occasionally require a special meeting, and you should move heaven and earth to be there. Once in a blue moon, your board will meet in executive session—behind closed doors, in total privacy. Only the trustees attend. No members of management are there unless they also happen to be trustees. A trusted general counsel could be present if the situation requires it. Executive sessions are held to discuss delicate subjects: ethical breaches, improper conduct by a manager, impending bad publicity, a lawsuit just filed. One example I endured is indelibly etched in my mind: a venerable private school with a shining reputation had two sets of parents claim that a teacher was guilty of sexual misconduct with students. Plural. Try that one on for size.

14
A crash course in committees

COMMITTEES

Most of the work of big and mature or sophisticated non-profit boards is performed at the committee level. The reasons are the time constraints on the board meetings, frequently due to the large size of the board, and the need for someone—not the entire board—to bore into enough detail to get the job done.

Some basic committees for boards of almost any size are as follows.

NOMINATING

The nominating committee is the most important committee because the continuation of the quality of the board is in its hands. Managers of the nonprofit organization are not normally involved in selection of new board members.

The nominating committee must constantly seek out fresh, generally younger, more interested, and *interesting* board members who will, in turn, attract similar people.

Maintaining the quality of a nonprofit board reminds me of caring for apple trees. You must prune regularly, fertilize (with interest by the existing members), and cultivate the new growth. Three years of neglect on any of these processes and you can lose the fruit-bearing quality of the tree. You get small, gnarled, uninteresting apples.

EXECUTIVE

The executive committee is empowered to act when the full board cannot. It can also assist in setting the agenda for board meetings to make them more productive. It is most often composed of the board's current officers.

This committee may not be important for years at a time in a nonprofit organization, but all of a sudden it can become the lifeline to sanity and good judgment in a crisis. Membership on the executive committee reminds me of military service: months and even years of tedium, broken by occasional moments of stark terror.

DEVELOPMENT

Show me a nonprofit organization without a development committee to seek funding, and I will show you one without a sense of its own direction. Exceptions include private family foundations, which by design receive all their money from the family, and boards that are publicly funded. The development committee provides leadership for securing financial support for the organization, taking charge of the activities that bring contributions. Every board member should serve on the development committee for at least two years to gain an understanding of what the tough job of fund-raising is like.

FINANCE

Some trustees must pay special attention to the money side of the organization. The functions of the finance committee are clear: oversee and plan the budget, be familiar with the accounting and control systems of the organization, follow financial activities on a regular basis, and keep the board fully informed.

SPECIAL

There are a number of committees with names and charges that may relate only to a particular organization and the cause it serves. Examples are buildings and grounds for a school or college, membership for a church or synagogue, and human resources or any other special area that concerns a board. Fit the committees to the size and special function of your board.

A FINAL WORD

Too many committees, like too many cooks, can spoil things. Create only a few. A trustee should serve on one committee only. At least that's the best way, though in rare cases a trustee could take on two committees. Be aware that you can wear out a trustee with too much committee work in addition to board meetings. Please watch out for yourself. Learn to say "No, thank you."

15

Spreading the word

COMMUNICATION

Boards of trustees of nonprofit organizations rarely communicate with the people they represent: donors and recipients.
It is an oddity of the system. It is a mistake.

The president of the board should send a letter once or twice a year to all persons involved directly with the organization: donors to its cause, recipients of its services, and also its employees. The letter should be brief—two or three paragraphs, all on one page—with the simple purpose of informing people of major events.

The letter is from the entire board, so the ending should read, "On behalf of the Board of Trustees," followed by the signature of the president.

What does the letter say? Again, it recaps major events only. Examples:

For a symphony orchestra: construction of a new symphony hall, with information on the major donors, the cost, and the timetable for opening.

For a child-care center: new location, new person in charge, recitation of brief statistics on children served.

For a foundation: significant new grants given, board or other personnel changes.

Also, please never, ever forget those two simple words: *thank you.* There are few things that encourage the continued support of donors or enthusiasm of volunteers more than telling them that they are appreciated.

Be brief. Inform. Do *not* ask questions; this is a report of facts. Say thank you.

16

A snapshot of the ideal board

COMPOSITION ~ SELECTION

What should the board look like when you see it sitting as a whole? In order to have the optimum board composition, other factors besides individual qualifications must be considered. The criteria for all boards change over time as the organization's needs change. However, some criteria are basic to all boards at all times.

Age

The classic argument arises: wisdom through experience versus the freshness of youth. How often have we heard, "She's a little young, isn't she?" Or the reverse: "He's a little too old, don't you think?" Nonsense to both. Age should not be a barrier at either end.

To ensure the continuity of the organization, the preference will usually be to seek younger people. And how do you get these younger people? Simple, if you don't mind a little work. Review the qualities you need in a trustee, and seek out a fresh individual who possesses them. Then ask that person to serve.

Nonprofit boards, however, often miss the opportunity to enlist older people who may have both the time and the money to assist them. Some people are better at seventy than others are at forty. The trick is finding the right ones and keeping an open mind about age. But remember that you always want a balance in the ages represented on your board.

Gender

There should no longer be any need for a discussion on this topic. The problem is, nonetheless, that in certain situations—incredibly—the subject of women still causes debate. The argument is always raised: "We can't find women with experience." Horsefeathers. Then just get some women without the experience, but get some. This argument that the supply cannot fill the demand must be overcome, and the way to do it is simple: just do it. All it takes is determination.

DIVERSITY

Racial, socio-economic, and ethnic diversity are mandatory for any nonprofit board that hopes to maintain a meaningful role in its community. Every board must include people of various backgrounds to get feedback on its work and inspiration for new projects from ALL of the people it represents. Such a policy not only follows the legal and moral concepts of today's world, but also is just common sense.

The vast majority of nonprofit boards are way ahead of any other segment of society. Business boards do not reflect their constituency in the same way that nonprofit boards do. I remember shamelessly forcing the issue on a business board by saying in an open meeting, "You don't discriminate against your customers, do you?" There was a blank stare. "Well," I said, "you want everyone to buy your products, don't you?" We got the needed representation on the board.

Boards are beginning to make room for the people most affected by their decisions. Twenty years ago I argued that faculty and students should be represented on the board of an independent school. I lost. So did the organization. But doesn't having a musician on the orchestra board make perfect sense?

Having a single, working mother on the board of the child-care center? You don't have to stop there. In considering diversity for your board, learn to think outside the box. Didn't you ever color outside the lines as a child? Here is your adult chance.

Marketing experience

No matter what a nonprofit organization does, at least one trustee should have a strong marketing background. We once lived in an age where the sizzle sold the steak. Now, of course, it's a menu of white fish and steamed vegetables. But the point is the same: the element of selling is still present, and we deny it at our peril. It is basic. Besides, marketing people are generally young and sharp, alive with both energy and ideas.

Technology experience

Someone with strong technical experience should be sitting around every nonprofit board table as a voting member.

What does that mean? It means that each board should have someone who understands the technology of the contemporary world: chips, computers, cellular phones, genetic engineering, whatever—someone who *uses* the newest technology all the time, ahead of the rest of us. They're the ones who were using e-mail and Web sites before we even knew what they were.

No, they need not know how everything works, but they must understand the vocabulary and potential. Technology is an ever-changing part of our daily lives. Accordingly, the requirement for such an individual on the board is fundamental. (Aha! Now we'll get younger people!) But heaven help anyone whose pager or cell phone goes off during a meeting.

THE FIVE HOOKS

These five hooks—a balance in ages, a balance in genders, someone with marketing savvy, someone strong on technology, and a broadly diverse membership—are sufficient to build your board around. Each nonprofit will add to this list depending on its field of interest or the stage in the life of the organization. Caveat: Don't develop too many additional criteria. You may get more hooks than you want.

17

The truth about trustee elections

Do you think the audiences or the musicians or the donors of a symphony orchestra elect the board? Don't be silly. Almost all nonprofit boards are self-perpetuating. They reelect themselves, or cause themselves to be reelected. Existing trustees select new trustees.

"So what?" you ask. "So boards of trustees elect and reelect themselves. Why should I care?"

Maybe you shouldn't, but I think you might consider the situation—especially if you are a trustee of such an organization. While there is no better way to keep a nonprofit board going than to let it select its own members, you need to be aware of the dangers that can arise from that environment. It is raw power, and Lord Acton's dictum that "Power corrupts, and absolute power corrupts absolutely" applies.

So what do you do? At the very least, examine your own motives for being a trustee. Resign if your motives are not what you feel they should be. Follow the old maxim "To thine own self be true, and . . . thou canst not then be false to any man." Ponder the question not only when you are elected the first time, but also each time you are reelected. Yes, you get to vote for yourself. The nominating committee presents its slate of people, and its recommendation is voted up or down. Bang! In two minutes it's over.

Persons you don't want

We've already talked about the qualities expected in a trustee and about the various sorts of people that a board needs. But what about the people a board doesn't need, those who might actually damage the organization?

The only people who should clearly be excluded from non-profit and public boards are those who are there for their own aggrandizement. Their work may be good, but our experience is that often they quit just when you need them. Or they may stay on the board but stop doing the work, and even skip meetings.

It's very hard to discern the motives of people before you work with them and see them perform. As a consequence, every organization can end up with people motivated for themselves, not for the common cause. There is no litmus test for motives, so we tend to take people at face value.

Despite the difficulty, beware of both men and women who seek and accept membership on any and all boards. They are often just collecting lapel pins as a sign of status. They are like those men of a century ago, accumulating ornaments for their watch fobs, or like women of a generation or two ago, gathering charms for their bracelets.

The head of one blue-chip organization on whose board I had served for a good while kept raising a particular person's name for board membership. I knew this person. The nominee was capable but sought membership on boards only for self-aggrandizement—and, by golly, was collecting them all over town. Boy, did this person push. Finally, after our CEO's third attempt to win approval for the nominee, which I deflected in the nominating committee, I took the CEO aside. "I feel so strongly that this person is not your style, not for us," I said, "that if this nominee comes, I go—and I don't want to." We laughed together, and we both blushed. Yes, I was overly aggressive, but I had to make my point. "Well," he responded, "what can I say? That settles it." Politics? Of course. It is everywhere, but so are pushy people. Push back.

18
Tenure: How long is long enough?

The basics really never change, and this is never more true
than in the case of the tenure of board members. There are
two simple rules:

1. HAVE TERMS.
2. LIMIT THE NUMBER OF TERMS.

These truths apply to all nonprofit organizations.

Board members, you see, are not like old soldiers. They
rarely, if ever, just fade away. Instead, you have to set limits
and, by doing so, retire each member eventually. It must be
done for the good of the organization, and if the limits are
established and known, ill feeling is eliminated.

Many trustees eventually leave boards on their own, without
the push of term limits. This is because nonprofit organizations often wear out the good people, and because the smart
trustees know when to go, as times change. But other trustees
need a little help finding the door. A trustee who stays too
long may begin arriving late to meetings, nodding off, sometimes leaving early, failing to do the homework. He or she
is only warming a chair and can poison the fine broth being
created by the other trustees.

A term of three years makes sense, and a limit of three terms does, too. Often it takes a year to become comfortable on the board, and even one full term to understand what it is all about. Two three-year terms seems too few, especially for an effective trustee. A total of three terms seems to work about right.

Some nonprofits have a provision that permits a retired trustee to be reelected to the board after being off for at least one year. Our experience is that under those circumstances this is a harmless provision, due to the fact that retired trustees almost never accept reelection—because by that time, they have moved on with their lives, as they should.

TENURE

19

How to get on a board

Since you're reading this handbook, you are probably already on a board or have been selected to fill a board seat. But for folks who still aspire to membership on a nonprofit board, either for the first time or in addition to the board they already serve on, here are some pointers.

The rules are the same for winning membership on a very high percentage of the boards of nonprofit organizations—and the rules get results.

DECIDE

Decide that sitting on the board of a nonprofit organization is what you really want, and decide why. Examine your motives. Choose the specific nonprofit you want to serve. Focus.

Wishers—the world is full of them, but if they are just wishers, they are not board members. "Oh, I wish I could be on the board at church," or "I wish I could sit on the school board," or "I wish I could get invited to join the music board." Understand that like most things in life worth doing, securing a board membership is up to you and no one else.

You decide what you want. At that moment, you take command.

WORK

Volunteer. All the time.

Let your interest be known by demonstrating it. Attend the public meetings. Attend the performances and all the functions: the auctions, the rummage sales. Buy the raffle tickets. Be alert. Be enthusiastic.

While attending everything, you will find that the work is there for the willing. There is generally little or no discrimination about who does it. Successful volunteering requires only knowing that the work is there, being willing to work, and applying honest effort once you get assigned the task.

How?

PERSIST

You will be offered a job. It will be a dirt job, quite possibly
one that no one else wants. You could be assigned to a small
committee to study the effects of the rainfall on supplies for
the water district. Or you could be asked to help sort through
the clothes and pots and pans given to the rummage sale.
You will be asked to work at undesirable hours, to work alone,
to stay up all night. Whatever. No one said it would be
glamorous.

Someday, somewhere, at a time and place unknown to you,
one person will say to another, "How about Paula [that's you]
as a board member?"

"Well, she certainly does love the theater."

"And she works like a Trojan. She never complains."

You've suddenly become a candidate.

USE CONNECTIONS DISCREETLY . . . IF AT ALL

Yes, of course, connections help. All towns are, ultimately,
small towns—even New York, Chicago, and Los Angeles. So if
you know someone connected with the board you're aiming for,
yes, it helps. But again, let me stress that a board seat can also
come to you through work, persistence, and passion.

How do you use a connection? Delicately. Obliquely.
Or not at all. If you do, simply let it be known that you are
interested and let your attributes say the rest for you.
Do not push. Be patient.

Don't overrate money

Sure, it counts. Give big bucks and you are bound to get attention. But if you do get asked to join a board solely because of your giving, and you think that is all the group wants, you will not be successful. Sure, the board wants your gift of money, but it also wants the gifts of your judgment and time at board meetings. Some of the new, young technology millionaires do not yet understand this concept. About 99 percent of them think a check discharges their responsibility. Wrong. They need to learn to give time and thought as well. We can assist them by asking them to be board members, not just donors.

Big contributors will clearly be sought after. However, this is far from the only way to join a board. Unless you are a truly stupendous giver, you probably won't get there on money alone. A trustee must give two of the three W's: work, wealth, and wisdom. My editor says this is a dated reference. Maybe, but this old saw still cuts—and sharply.

"Can she give?"

Oh, yeah, that scary question is out there. If it is an organization that depends in part on contributions of money, that question will be asked about you as a prospective trustee. Not to worry. The response more often than not will be:

"Give? You bet. Herself. Time. Work. And she's smart."

Few organizations are dumb enough to think they can survive on money alone. Otherwise they wouldn't be around. You will be invited to the board.

ACCEPT

Do not be modest.

"I'm pleased," you say. "I accept. I promise that I will work harder than ever and make the organization pleased that it asked me." That is what you say. Just speak from your heart.

On pain of death, you never say, "Well, I'd like to, but you know I can't give very much."

You say, "Great. When do I start?"

PERFORM

PERFORM

Once on the board, you do not slow down, you do not slack
off, you do not bask in your tub, sprinkled with the oil of your
delight. You keep going, now more persistent than before.

You are proving your worth. You are becoming one of the
best board members the organization has ever had. With your
enthusiasm and energy, the board will turn to you more and
more, following the wise dictum "If you want a job done well,
give it to a busy person."

Be busy, be active—but also be something that a lot of
trustees, for some inexplicable reason, stop being. Be smart.
Think about the organization. Reflect. Concentrate.
Ask questions.

You will discover that boards are like the Old Testament:
a lot of begats. One board is forever begetting another, which
begets one more—and they all want only the sharpest and very
best trustees. That's you. You will run out of interest, time,
energy, and life before those boards run out of their desire for
you. You'll find that your performance on one board will be
the single most important factor determining whether you will
be invited to join another board.

20
How to leave a board

Yes, there are even rules for *leaving* a board. They're simple ones.

LEAVE EARLY

If you're fortunate, your board will have established terms
and term limits. Even if they do, leave the board earlier than
anyone expects you to.

You certainly never want to be asked to leave or to have the
rest of the board wishing you were gone. Consequently, not
merely do you leave before anyone expects you to, but you leave
before the thought even crosses anyone's mind.

Like a few great athletes, or even some great actors, leave at
the peak, at the top of your game. You will be remembered as
you want to be. Instead of looking at you and thinking, "He's
an old has-been," people will say, "He was a great trustee!"

LEAVE QUICKLY

Make your decision and get it over with. Inform the president
of the board and then announce your decision—by letter—
and graciously disappear. Perhaps you sit through one meeting
after you've announced your departure, but not more.

Do not expect anything when you leave. Nonprofit boards are simply not that smart in honoring years of work. They are learning, but slowly.

Many years ago I solicited a former trustee for an annual gift. He said no.

"C'mon," I said, "you served a long time, did a superb job."

He paused for a good while.

"Bill, listen. I did serve for fourteen long years. You know what happened at my last meeting? As it ended, as everyone was getting up and talking and heading for the door, the president said, 'Oh yes, it's Ted's last meeting. Thanks, Ted.' One or two people clapped. I got in my car, and driving home I thought, *Good grief. That's all, after fourteen years.*"

I apologized to him on behalf of the board. Then I went out and bought a nice plaque for each of the current trustees who were about to retire. And I got one for Ted, too.

Nonprofit boards are truly smart when they honor trustees who retire or resign after serving the organization. Not only is it proper and polite to do so, but it's also good business. Be sure your nonprofit corporation presents a token of appreciation to a departing trustee. Make it something substantial: a wall plaque, a paperweight, a framed picture with an engraved inscription, bookends, a chair—something that will last. Do it, and your organization will have a friend and loyal supporter for life.

21
Have fun

If you believe in the cause, if you like the folks you're working with, and if you feel you are making a difference, you're going to have fun as a trustee. If you're not having fun and don't feel valued, get out. Life is too short.

WELL SO LONG

22
Addendum

Since the first printing of this guidebook, in 1999, nonprofit organizations and their boards have come under increasing public scrutiny and pressure to be more accountable and transparent.

At the same time, boards have found identifying, recruiting, and training new trustees to be a major challenge.

Although the concepts presented in the original book remain for the most part tried-and-true, boards and nonprofit CEOs have redoubled their efforts to achieve success and satisfaction in their work. This addendum attempts to touch on some of the ways CEOs and boards are working together to reach their goals.

23
The changing relationship between the CEO and the board

Historically, boards have stayed out of the details of running the organization. The reasoning was based on the belief that chief executives manage the day-to-day operations, while boards make policy.

Today's reality is that few nonprofits can risk having the chief executive divorced from policy development or contrarily the board from policy implementation. To achieve success and satisfaction today requires close teamwork between the board and the chief executive. In short, governance works best as a partnership in which the work and accomplishments are shared. The board and chief executive together set policy and implement it. Who does what, when, in the implementation process, is hammered out and agreed on.

Power is shared by the CEO and the board. Both put aside egos and exercise informed leadership to advance the mission. This takes work to accomplish, and as with any other sustainable and positive relationship, nothing should be taken for granted.

In reality, no chief executive or board necessarily has all the answers. By working collaboratively as a team, they can bring to bear their collective wisdom and experience in addressing institutional priorities.

It is of great importance that trustees have a positive, constructive relationship with the chief executive. Organizations that achieve this are most often very successful by any measure. When CEOs and board members have a high level of engagement and challenge one another in productive ways, good things result.

In too many instances, trustees are unable to fulfill their potential, not because they are unsure and confused about their role, but because they are frustrated and dissatisfied. The questions they are asking are "Am I making a difference?" "Does this work matter?" "Is this really worth my time?"

Today's entrepreneurial trustee demands being "hands on." A growing number of organizations, even those with robust staffs, now encourage trustee participation in the day-to-day work of the organization, including the heretofore taboo areas of personnel and program development. The results, in many instances, have been dramatic. Trustees come away with a better understanding of why they are there and what a positive difference they can make.

24

Board size, structure, and composition

Standing committees are permanent and members are appointed for designated terms. These committees are responsible for a range of issues such as finance, development, and programs. The characteristics of work, wisdom, wealth, and wallop are all important ingredients to ensure a highly functioning board and committee structure. Organizations should be looking for team players, individuals who have intellectual firepower, street smarts, a tolerance for ambiguity, and the courage to ask tough questions, and who delight in the interchange of ideas.

The board committee (often the Executive Committee) responsible for trustee recruitment is increasingly considered by many organizations to be the most important committee of all. It's where you want your most experienced, supportive, and respected trustees.

Ad hoc committees and task forces allow the board to focus attention on narrower matters of importance that the full board cannot take the time to address. They have a specific charge from the board or executive committee and sunset when they have completed their work.

The typical board size is fifteen to twenty-one. There is a strong argument for a smaller board, six to nine, which allows for more active engagement and a greater sense of ownership and accountability for ensuring that the organization achieves its mission and objectives. On a large board, often, an executive committee will be appointed and will meet more frequently in between full board meetings.

Boards should engage in a thorough review annually, ensuring that their size, structure, and composition are designed to maximize effective governance and transparency.

There is no one size fits all. The most important point to evaluate is whether the organization has been able to fulfill its goals and expectations and keep the active and passionate engagement of trustees.

25
Deploy your assets

Make sure that you as a trustee take the time to think about how your organization can have the biggest impact on achieving the mission. Too often, trustees fail to apply the wisdom, experience, and skills they bring to the board. It works best when the chief executive comes to the board for counsel and advice well before any formal request for board action. This is where trustees and executive staff, working together, can frame the important questions and consider multiple solutions. It's often the time when the most creative and dynamic thinking takes place.

This is not familiar ground for many chief executives and boards. You will need to discover and practice new ways of working together. Change is rarely comfortable. Stress, ambiguity, disagreement, and resistance are predictable. However, confronting complex institutional challenges can enrich the work of the chief executive and board. In short, the board has greater impact and value when it deploys all its assets—intellectual, financial, and social—in helping the organization achieve its highest potential.

So, be prepared to get out and stay out of your comfort zone. You'll find that real benefits occur for the institution.

26
Accountability and finances

Make sure you have the financial information you need to keep your organization on track and accountable to your constituents, as well as to maintain tax-exempt and corporate status with federal and state agencies. Your organization must keep accurate and current financial records.

Ensure that the organization has strong internal accounting systems and that management will produce timely and accurate income and expense statements, balance sheets, and budget status reports in advance of board meetings. Require confirmation from those responsible that all required filings are up-to-date and employee withholding taxes and insurance premiums are paid on time. Monitor fund-raising to ensure that goals are realistic and reports are accurate. Verify that contributed funds are used in accordance with the donors' wishes.

Remember, you are the link between your organization and those it serves.

27

Risk management

Simply put, a nonprofit organization cannot operate success-fully without taking risks. Risk is an essential part of an entrepreneurial organization. The board needs to weigh the inherent risks of the organization and any decisions they or staff consider to accomplish their mission. Risk management provides the necessary framework for trustees to understand what the risks are and then to empower the CEO to make wise choices in dealing with these risks. Risk management focuses on an organization's most important assets: human, physical, income, and reputation. In reality, risk management frees your organization to take more—not less—risk. It puts you, not the risk, in charge, so you'll have no surprises. In many situations, inaction and failure to take a positive, calculated action can put your organization at a greater risk of "dying a slow death."

28

Raising the bar with Sarbanes-Oxley

In 2002, Congress enacted Sarbanes-Oxley to address exposures identified by the Enron and other corporate-sector scandals. While most of the Act addresses publicly traded companies, two requirements affect all organizations, including nonprofits.

1. Whistleblower Protection. All organizations must have a documented, formal process for both following up on complaints about unethical or illegal conduct and protecting the people who voice these complaints.

2. Document Retention and Periodic Destruction Policy. All organizations must have a written document that identifies policies and procedures for retaining key administrative and financial documents and conform to the guidelines it sets out.

Additional recommended policies are to have an independent and competent audit committee, certified financial statements, and a conflict of interest policy, specifically with regard to loans to directors and executives.

29
Taking on debt

In some instances, a board taking on debt can be a smart business decision for the organization. It can be an inexpensive and long-term form of acquiring capital for asset acquisitions and capital projects. Avoid incurring debt at all costs to fund normal operations. The important filter is that the debt will, in every respect, advance the mission of the organization.

Boards who vote to incur debt should have realistic and conservative assumptions about how the organization will repay the debt. Sometimes a board making a decision not to take on debt may actually increase the risk of failure for the organization. In all cases, make sure the debt can be easily serviced. Don't forget to explore the possibility of tax-exempt bond financing from state and local government entities. With lower interest rates and the attractiveness of debt to lenders and investors, you may be able to build sooner than expected. Often, there is value in hiring a third party to assess an organization's exposure. You'll need to have a plan in place to meet debt-service payments. In the case of a school, it may mean a substantial increase in tuition and greater expectations for charitable contributions. Ask yourselves whether your constituency will respond favorably.

30

The Uniform Prudent Investor Act

The Uniform Prudent Investor Act requires that nonprofit
board members and others carefully assess investment goals,
risks versus returns, and proper diversification of assets.
Hence, under the Uniform Prudent Investor Act, a trust's
entire investment portfolio is considered when determining
the prudence of an individual investment. Diversification
is explicitly required as a duty for prudent fiduciary investing.
No category or type of investment is deemed inherently
imprudent. The primary determinants are the account's
purposes and the beneficiaries' needs.

However, while a fiduciary is permitted to develop flex-
ibility in a portfolio, speculation and outright risk-taking are
not sanctioned by the Act. Hence, a fiduciary runs the risk
of possible liability and criticism for failed investment.

In today's complex investment world, an outside adviser
is recommended for any organization considering investment
as a means to maintaining and increasing its asset base.

31
Avoid self-dealing

Boards must guard against unauthorized self-dealing, that is involving the corporation in any transaction in which the trustee has a material, or significant, financial interest without proper approval. The self-dealing rules and proper approval requirements can arise in many different kinds of transactions, such as the purchase or sale of corporate property, investment of corporate funds, or the payment of corporate fees or compensations. In most cases the interest of the trustee must be disclosed prior to any vote, and only disinterested members of the board may vote on any given proposal.

Sanctions for self-dealing range from payment of penalties to the IRS to revocation of the organization's tax-exempt status.

32

Succession plans

The board must create a succession plan for the organization's chief executive. Things happen expectedly and unexpectedly. Your chief executive should nurture leadership within the organization so if he or she departs, the board is prepared to hire a new chief executive from within or from outside the organization.

Together we'll make it grow!

33

Research

Many nonprofits play a key role in conducting and funding research in the medical and health-related sciences, the natural and social sciences, and engineering.

Most trustees have no idea about research. They tend to believe the "great man/great woman" theory. That is, you give some smart scientist a grant and he or she "discovers things," as if they were just lying around waiting to be discovered. In reality, the best ideas about research often come from outside the discipline, from folks who do not know what is "impossible" and who have the freedom to think "outside the box" when developing hypotheses and setting goals. Trustees need to have an "outcomes focused" approach and philosophy so they can be part of pulling the human and financial resources together to make things happen. Hold researchers accountable for the expenditure of all funds. It is not all about raising and spending money and continuing the academic careers of researchers. Ask yourself the question: Are our resources being spent in ways that ensure science will lead rapidly to new products that are good for patients and good for the economy?

Great research starts with key questions such as what does success look like and how will we share our results with our key donors and the public? So, four key points to consider:

■ Failure is a given. Without it you are not trying hard enough.

■ Research is a process that feeds on itself. Clearly define expectations and objectives at the start of the process. Then, adjust plans, if need be, as you go along. Think big, start small, and move fast.

■ Young investigators can be much more productive than senior ones, so keep a mix.

■ The best research leads the field and changes the way things are done.

Some final thoughts. Expect the unexpected and understand that, as a trustee of a nonprofit that funds or conducts research, you have the responsibility to ask lots of questions and to get answers that are in easy-to-understand language. Be aware that some donors will want to retain title to both equipment and certain intellectual property. Be flexible in determining who should own what. Look for win-win opportunities for your researchers, your organization, and your donors. Remember, you and the CEO are accountable for ensuring that applicable research doesn't simply end up on the shelf, but is put to use to serve the greater good.

34

Simple tips for more effective meetings

Consider the use of a "consent agenda" to dispense with routine and uncontested items. A consent agenda does not require discussion or debate and includes such things as minutes from the last meeting, financial reports, dates of future meetings, and special resolutions. The consent agenda should be a part of your board mailing.

Use e-mail to increase board effectiveness. Circulate board materials, meeting agendas, committee reports, and proposals for major board action via e-mail in advance of meetings. At the board meeting, avoid oral presentations of routine reports that have previously been mailed to the board. Board members can then respond with comments and suggestions.

35

Board executive sessions

An "executive session" needs to be a regular part of every full board meeting. Your board will meet initially with the chief executive to discuss any issues they wish to consider without staff present. Then the board will excuse the chief executive and meet in total privacy with only trustees.

Beyond sensitive governance issues, executive sessions give trustees a chance to talk candidly among themselves about how they can better support the chief executive or to iron out differences of opinion among themselves or with the chief executive. It is also a time when the board can look candidly at its performance and ask the tough questions of one another: Are we working well as a team? If not, why not? What do we need to do individually and collectively to improve performance? When there is a climate of trust, it's far easier to make course corrections.

36

The board executive committee

An executive committee is particularly useful if you have a board of more than fifteen members. The executive committee is empowered by the full board to act on its behalf. It can also assist in setting the agenda for board meetings to make them more productive. It is most often composed of the board's current officers. The purpose of the executive committee is time efficiency. Solicit input when appropriate on complex issues or invite selected trustees to participate.

One warning: keep the full board informed of all the work of the executive committee. Distribute minutes *immediately.* Keep your executive committee meetings open so that any trustees can attend if they so desire. Everyone on the board needs to feel involved, and the perception that there is a clique of decision-makers can erode the sense of ownership you want all trustees to have.

37

Trustee voting and the chief executive

The organization's chief executive or executive director should not be an official voting member of the board. It confuses the governance relationship. The CEO works for and reports to the board. Conflicts of interest can and often do arise. Permitting your chief executive to serve as a nonvoting, ex-officio board member can eliminate this problem.

38

Chief executive and board performance indicators

Establish clear performance indicators, sometimes called dashboards, of success for your chief executive and board linked
to your strategic plan. This enables board members to get a
snapshot of your organization to see how it's doing and where
the holes might be. Dashboards might include hits on a
Web site compared to last year or contributions year-to-date
compared with last year at the same time. A single-page
dashboard could be included in the board materials prior to
every board meeting.

Review progress at every meeting. The development of these
key indicators will keep you focused on what matters most.

" Thanks for your impant. i value your wisdom,
experience and support, because without it,
the task facing us would be difficult "

39

Recognition

Being a board member in today's environment is demanding. Most trustees put in extraordinary amounts of time and money. While most find their work to be satisfying, being acknowledged by others for a job well done can be very gratifying. The same can be said for donors and staff, whose contributions often are taken for granted. Take the time to honor those who have toiled above and beyond for your organization. Acknowledgment of exemplary performance can be a part of every board meeting. You will be rewarded by increased enthusiasm and commitment and will have made lifelong friends.

Acknowledgments

We wish to acknowledge, most gratefully, and express our deep appreciation to the many people who have made this project possible:

First and foremost, praise and thanks to Jolene and Bruce McCaw—this project would not have been possible without their enthusiasm, input, support, and encouragement.

To our numerous nonprofit colleagues, thank you for your insights and recommendations. Thank you, Jamie Heywood and Greg Simons, for your input on research. We are grateful to BoardSource for their outstanding publications on governance. Special thanks to Richard P. Chait, William P. Ryan, and Barbara E. Taylor for your groundbreaking work in *Governance as Leadership.* You have inspired our thinking about how to achieve high-performing boards.

Thanks to our editors, Don Graydon, Carolyn Margon, Debra Jensen, and Judy Gouldthorpe; our designer, Paul Langland; and our publisher, Barry Provorse, for their perceptive insights and guidance throughout the long process.

And thanks as well to our individual spouses and families, whose loving support, unflagging encouragement, and patience have made all the difference.

WILLIAM GOLDING's legacy includes his contribution as a trustee of ten different nonprofit corporations, including a major symphony orchestra, a small day-care center, a church, two schools, and a big-city library foundation. He served as the CEO of two midsize corporations following a successful career in law. An earlier book, *What It Takes* (Putnam's), about how to become and perform as a CEO, was critically acclaimed. Volumes of his poetry were prepared for publication, and he completed work on a novel prior to his death in 2004. He lived with his wife on an island in Puget Sound near Seattle.

CRAIG STEWART has spent over thirty-six years in the nonprofit sector. He has lectured and written on philanthropy and on the role of trustees of nonprofit organizations. He is the president and trustee of The Bruce & Jolene McCaw Family Foundation in Bellevue and has served and continues to serve on a number of nonprofit boards, including Talaris Institute. He lives with his wife in Edmonds, Washington.

TEDROWE WATKINS, an entrepreneur and philanthropist, has volunteered on nonprofit boards for decades. A former Marine pilot, he has also served as the CEO of a private business. He is now retired and pursuing his hobby of painting while dividing his time between homes in Montana and Southern California.